Lil' Champs play it SMART

The Playful Way to Learn Social Skills and Manners

This book is dedicated to my beautiful lil'champs that play it SMART.

Suzanne M. Wind

This book belongs to: _____

First Printing 2015

ISBN: 13 978-0692472200
ISBN: 10 0692472207

**ModernGrace Publishing
Greenwich, CT**

thesmartplaybook@gmail.com
www.thesmartplaybook.com
facebook/thesmartplaybook
Twitter@suzanne_wind

Order Information: Special discounts are available on quantity purchase by corporation, associations, educations and others. For details contact the publisher at the above email address.

CONTENTS

A NOTE TO THE COACHES 01

LET THE GAMES BEGIN 02

GAME PLAN #1 – SOCIAL SKILL BASICS 03
- I Have Good Manners
- The Golden Rule
- First Impressions
- Be Kind
- The Race to Clean Up
- Look Up and Show Your Eyes
- Say Hello
- The Great Handshake
- Use Your Smile
- Telephone Smarts
- Play dates
- Thank-You Notes
- Grateful for Gifts
- I Love Good Sportsmanship
- Way to Go!

GAME PLAN #2 – MEALTIME MANNERS 21
- I Have Good Table Manners
- Pre-Dinner Prep
- A SMART Mealtime Story
- Finding Your Way
- The Table Setting Game Plan
- Share a Dinner Funny
- What's On Your Plate
- On the Dinner Table
- A SMART Word Story
- A Napkin with Style
- King or Queen of the Table
- Match Great Manners
- Lil' SMART Memory Game
- Mealtime Badge of Honor
- Way to Go!

GAME PLAN #3 – ART OF CONVERSATION 39
- Magic Word Hat
- Excuse Me Detective
- Match the Emotion
- I RICA You
- My Space
- Fumbles and Fillers
- Empathy Detective
- Talking Tennis Match
- Speak Up

- Listen Up
- Take Turns
- Voice Volume Control
- Mirror, Mirror on the Wall
- Way to Go!

GAME PLAN #4 – RESTAURANT BEHAVIOR 55
- The Dress Code
- A Fancy Closet
- Match the Clothes
- Here I Come
- Finger Food Detective
- My Favorite Foods
- Good Manners Detective
- What's On Your Menu
- How to Order Your Meal?
- A Joke For You
- A Special Date
- Way to Go!

GAME PLAN #5 – TECHNOLOGY TALK 67
- The Key to Computer Safety
- Be a Good Digital Citizen
- Good Digital Citizen Detective
- Finding My Tech Way
- Volume Control
- Hit the Pause Button, Please
- I Love Technology
- What Doesn't Belong?
- Take Care of Your Electronics
- A Tech Joke for You
- Balance Your time
- Way to Go!

BONUS! FAMILY GAME TIME 81
- The Polite Puppet
- A SMART Dice game
- SMART Meal Mission
- Good Manners Secret Agent
- Acts of Kindness Mission
- The Do or Don't Game
- Would You Rather...
- Magic Word Cards
- Guess the Emotion
- DIY Conversation Cards
- The Giggle Jar
- Make Your Own Crown
- Parent Book Suggestions to Read with Your Lil' Champ
- Parent SMART Checklist

➡️ A NOTE TO THE COACHES

(That means you, parents, educators and caretakers!)

Dear Coaches,

Learning manners and social skills at an early age is an important step in helping your child gain confidence, character, integrity and empathy. This book is set up in a game format to encourage your child to complete SMART challenges. Simple directions and engaging activities are geared toward helping your child stand out for all the RIGHT reasons. It is easy — have your child work page by page, following the tickets. Each time they complete a page, they should color in their ticket. Each activity page is a teachable moment to discuss appropriate behavior.

☑ Find a comfortable place where you and your child can work together.

☑ Offer praise and support for taking the challenges.

☑ Your child should color the ticket when they complete a page.

☑ Reward his or her work by tallying up tickets and offering a prize of your choosing in the beginning of each section.

☑ BONUS! Practice these skills with family games in the back of the book.

☑ Have fun!

⟶ LET THE GAMES BEGIN!

(Coaches, please read the game goals to your Lil'Champ.)

Welcome to the Play it SMART team! The SMART team is a group of Lil' Champs that knows how to stand out for all the RIGHT reasons. As an important member of this team, your job is to draw, write, and play games, all to learn the keys to having great friends, gaining respect from adults and growing into a kind and caring person. Are you ready?

Please keep track of how many tickets you can earn!

GAME PLAN #1 - SOCIAL SKILLS BASICS

GOAL:
Learn how to make good choices and how to act politely every day.

Coach, please read each statement aloud. Then have your child place a check in the box or color the box.

Player Mission:
- ☐ Treat people the way you want to be treated.
- ☐ Be kind and respectful to all.
- ☐ Be a great playdate.
- ☐ Give and accept gifts politely.
- ☐ Be a good sport.

Game Directions:
1. Take the challenges.
2. Find the ticket on the page and color the ticket when you have completed your mission.
3. At the end of a section, you win! Cash in for the reward chosen with your coach (an adult).

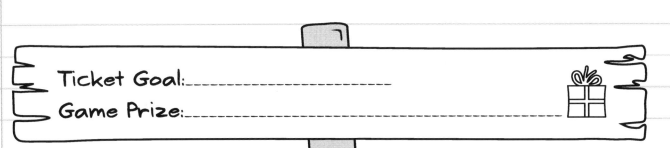

Ticket Goal:_____

Game Prize:_____

¡ HAVE GOOD MANNERS!

Ready to board the SMART bus? Connect the dots in alphabetical order and get your crown on.

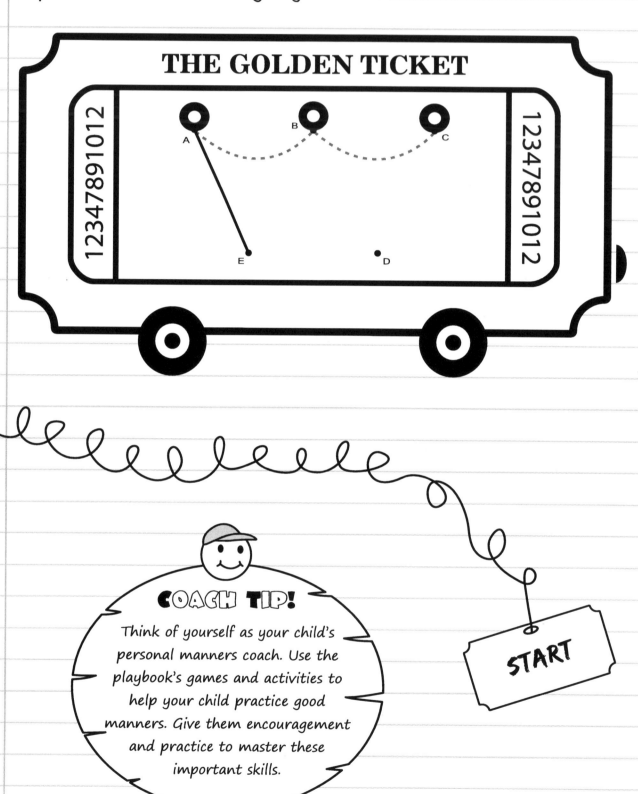

THE GOLDEN TICKET

12347891012

12347891012

A B C
E D

COACH TIP!

Think of yourself as your child's personal manners coach. Use the playbook's games and activities to help your child practice good manners. Give them encouragement and practice to master these important skills.

START

THE GOLDEN RULE

Treat people the way you would like to be treated. Please color your golden ticket and cut it out. Hang it in your room as a reminder.

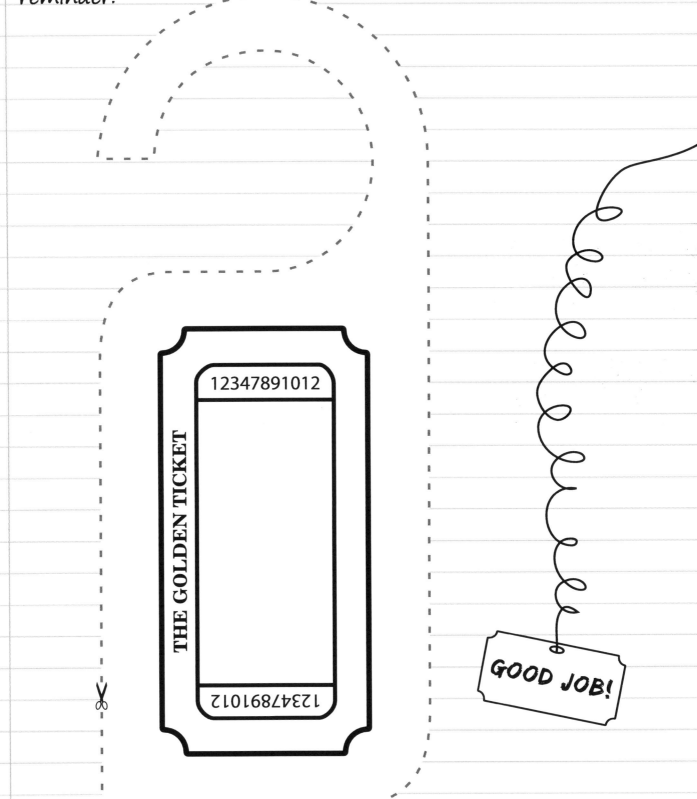

THE GOLDEN TICKET

12347891012

12347891012

GOOD JOB!

FiRST iMPRESSiONS

A first impression is what a person thinks of you the first time he meets you. You only get one chance, so make it BIG! Help find your way to a great first impression.

BE KIND

Please color this important word and remember to always be kind.

WAY TO GO!

COACH TIP!
Play the 'Act of Kindness Game' on page 91. It's a fun way to encourage your child to be considerate.

THE RACE TO CLEAN UP

Always clean up your mess. Ready, set, go!

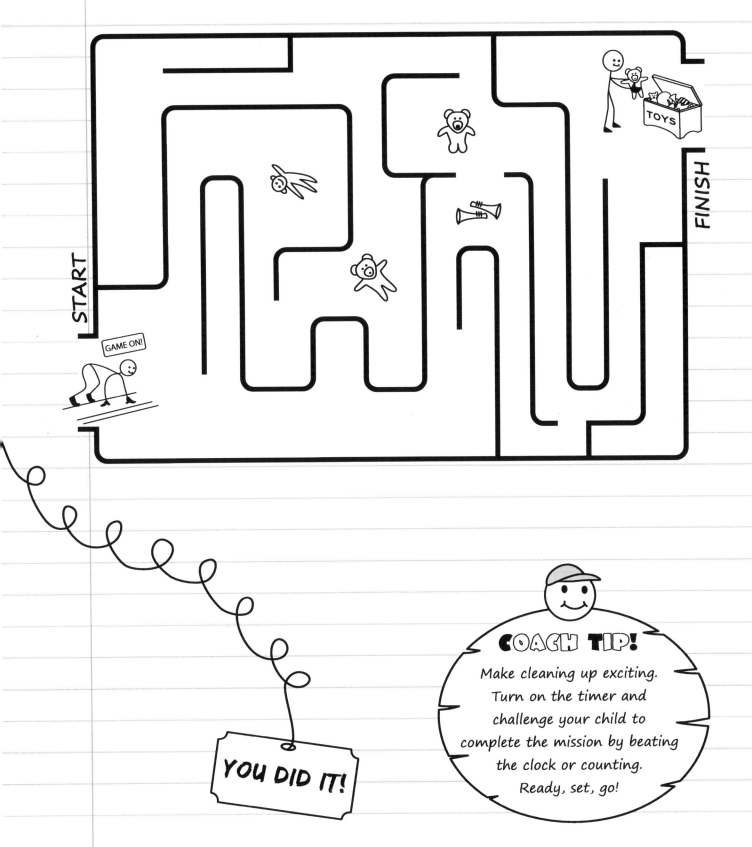

START

GAME ON!

FINISH

TOYS

YOU DID IT!

COACH TIP!

Make cleaning up exciting. Turn on the timer and challenge your child to complete the mission by beating the clock or counting. Ready, set, go!

LOOK UP AND SHOW YOUR EYES

Always look people in the eye when saying hello (even if you feel a little shy). Eye contact shows that you are **FRIENDLY** and **HONEST**. Color the large eyes. Make them bright and happy!

AWESOME!

COACH TIP!

Play the 'Great Stare-Down Challenge' and practice eye contact. Can you make your child laugh? Tell a story while looking your child straight in the eye. Who can tell the funniest story and make the other person look away from laughing?

SAY HELLO

Always say hello and use a person's name to show you care.
Fill in the blank:

Hi,_____!
(Name of a friend)

Hi,_____!
(Your name)

GREAT JOB!

THE GREAT HANDSHAKE

Stand tall and confident. Take a step forward and reach out your hand. Give a firm shake. Trace your hand here:

HIGH FIVE!

1. Stand Tall And Confident
2. Take A Step Forward
3. Reach Out Your Hand
4. Give A Firm Shake

COACH TIP!

Practice and encourage your child to shake someone's hand. Show them the difference between a firm shake and a loose, flimsy handshake.

USE YOUR SMILE

Your smile is a powerful tool. A big smile makes you look happy and confident. The more you smile the happier you will feel. Can you make a giant smiley face?

KEEP IT UP!

TELEPHONE SMARTS

Ready to call another Lil' Champ? Introduce yourself.
Ask politely to speak to your friend. Don't forget the
magic words. Fill in the blank.

Hi. This is_____.
(Your name)

May I please speak_____?

with_____
(Your friend's name)

Thank you.

My Phone Number is:_____
In an emergency I call: 911

ALMOST THERE

COACH TIP!

Help your Lil' Champ create
a phone book with important
numbers. Role play with a
pretend phone to teach
your child telephone
skills.

PLAY DATES

Be a good host or guest. A host makes everyone feel welcome and comfortable. A guest follows the house rules. Circle who is being a good host or guest.

Hello

Sharing

Friendly

Goodbye

Jumping

Grabbing

COACH TIP!

Role play with your child different scenarios at someone's house. Make it fun by exaggerating really good behavior and really bad behavior. Talk about the differences.

WOW!

THANK YOU NOTES

Writing a note lets a person know how much his or her kindness is appreciated. Help decorate the thank you card.

Dear_____,

Thank You

for

_____

_____

Your Name

COACH TIP!

Visit
www.thesmartplaybook.com
for a free thank you
note guide.

I'M IMPRESSED!

GRATEFUL FOR GIFTS ☺

Always say something positive when you receive a gift. Please color your gift.

i ♥ GOOD SPORTSMANSHIP

Always play fair and be polite. Good sportsmanship
is when teammates, opponents, coaches and officials
treat each other with respect. Ready for Tic Tac Toe?
Win or lose, please shake hands after the game.

ONE MORE!

WAY TO GO!

You are a star player! Trace the dotted lines and then color it in.

WOW! Coach, I earned _____ tickets!

(Count how many colored tickets you completed.)

You play it SMART

19

GAME PLAN #2 - MEALTIME MANNERS

GOAL:
We follow simple table manners to make mealtime enjoyable for all.

Coach, please read each statement aloud. Then have your child place a check in the box or color the box.

Player Mission:
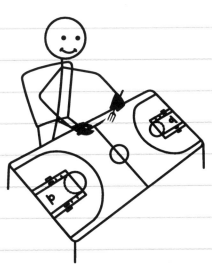

☐ Learn to help set the table.

☐ Eat with a fork or spoon.

☐ Behave politely at the table.

☐ Enjoy a nice meal with your family.

Game Directions:

1. Take the challenges.

2. Find the ticket on the page and color the ticket when you have completed your mission.

3. At the end of a section, you win! Cash in for the reward chosen with your coach (an adult).

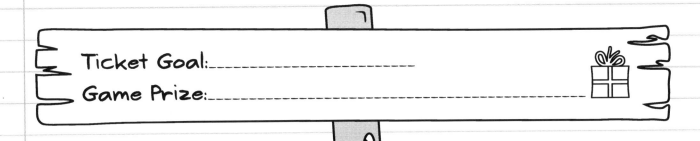

Ticket Goal:_____

Game Prize:_____

i HAVE GREAT TABLE MANNERS!

Always practice good table manners. Circle all good manners.

Place napkin on your lap.

Use your utensils, NOT your fingers.

No elbows on the table.

No bodily noises.

Good posture at the table.

No playing at the table.

START

COACH TIP!

Play the "Good Manner Secret Agent" game on page 89 to help your child practice these skills.

PRE-DINNER PREP

Before you eat, wash your hands and dress appropriately. What happens first? Write down the correct order of events labeling them with numbers 1—4.

A SMART MEALTIME STORY

Have a grown up help you read the story. Can you count how many ways Mia showed bad table manners?

Lil' Champ was excited to eat dinner at her friend Mia's house.

Dinner was ready and they washed their hands and sat down.

Mia grabbed the <u>spaghetti with her fingers</u> and then told

Lil' Champ a story <u>while spitting food.</u> She <u>reached</u>

<u>over her brother</u> to grab some more ketchup. Then she

used her <u>sleeve to wipe her mouth.</u> She grabbed the bread

from the basket and <u>stuffed it into her mouth.</u> Then when

she was done, she let out <u>a large BURP!</u>

Write down the number of bad manners:_____

KEEP IT UP!

24

FINDING YOUR WAY!

Find your way to good manners. Take the path to join the polite team.

THE TABLE SETTING GAME PLAN

Who are the players and the positions in a table setting? Help your mom or dad set the table tonight. Color the picture and use it as your guide.

The Players.......
MP - Main Plate
K - Knife
S - Spoon
D - Drink
N - Napkin
DF - Dinner Fork

N

DF

MP

D

K   S

COACH TIP!

Make table setting fun. Time your kids to see who can set it the fastest. Ready, set, go!

AWESOME!

SHARE A DINNER FUNNY!

Knock, Knock!
-Who's there?
Dishes
-Dishes who?
Dishes me, who are you?

COACH TIP!

Remember to keep practicing holding utensils. Young children are still working on their fine motor skills, so you can't expect them to hold a fork or spoon properly as well.

TOO FUNNY!

WHAT'S ON YOUR PLATE?

Please color your plate with delicious foods. Then help complete the puzzle by drawing a line to connect the right utensil to its place.

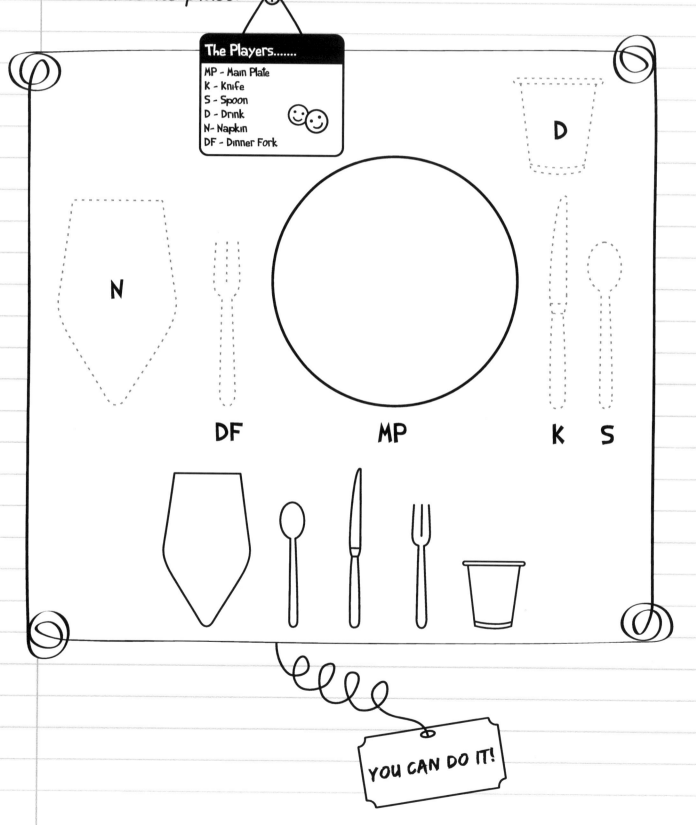

The Players.......
MP - Main Plate
K - Knife
S - Spoon
D - Drink
N- Napkin
DF - Dinner Fork

D

N

DF   MP   K   S

YOU CAN DO IT!

ON THE DINNER TABLE

Circle the items that don't belong on the table during meals.

COACH TIP!

Remind your child that toys do not belong at the dinner table.

EXCELLENT

A SMART WORD STORY

Have a grown up help you read the story. Circle the magic words.

Lil' Champ wanted a special snack, but his mom was talking to someone. He said, "**Excuse me**, Mom." She said, "Just a minute," so he patiently waited until she finished talking. Then his mom asked, "What would you like to eat?" "May I have animal crackers, **please**?" he said. She said, "**I'm sorry**, we don't have animal crackers. Would you like cheese and crackers instead?" "Yes, **please**!" Mom gave Lil' Champ his snack and he said, "**Thank you**, Mom." She said, "**You're welcome**".

Thank you

YES!

A NAPKIN WITH STYLE

Before eating, the napkin should be placed on your lap and used throughout the meal. Please connect the dots and then decorate your napkin.

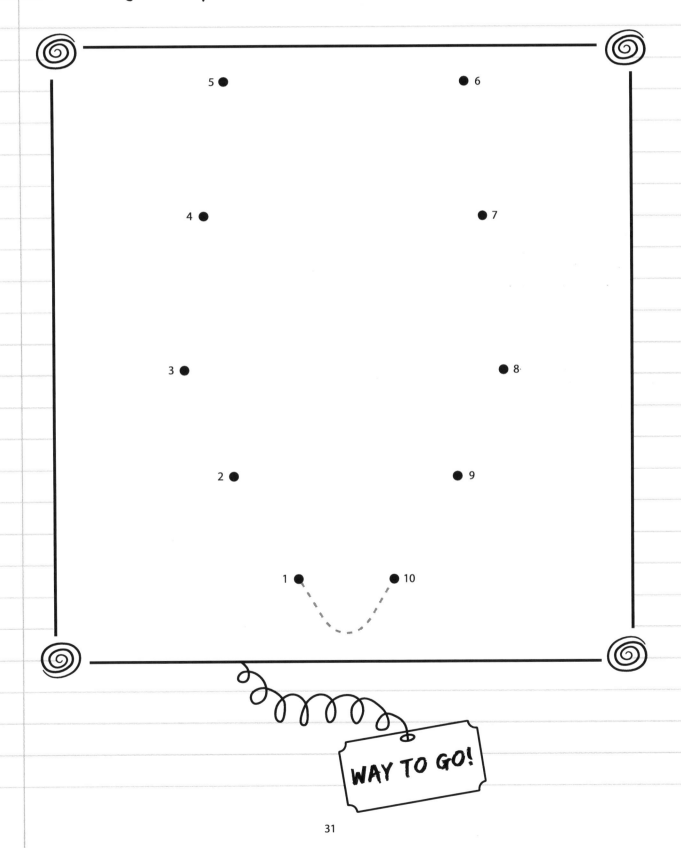

WAY TO GO!

KING OR QUEEN OF THE TABLE

Decorate your crowns. Are you ready for your royal meal?

COACH TIP!

See page 115 to make a crown for your child. Prepare a royal meal and have your child wear the crown.

YES!

MATCH GREAT MANNERS

Please draw a line to all matching good manners.

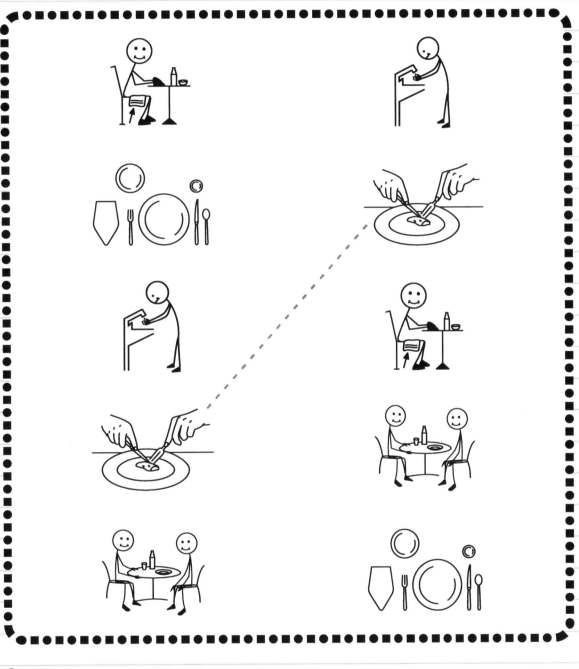

GREAT JOB!

LiL' SMART MEMORY GAME

Study this page for a minute. Then close the book. See how many things you can remember.

ONE MORE...

MEALTIME BADGE OF HONOR

What you'll need: scissors, markers and string.

Color and cut out your badge. Make a hole in the top of the badge. Pull a length of yarn or string through the hold. Tie both ends of the yarn together and make a necklace.

I HAVE GOOD TABLE MANNERS

YOU DID IT!

COACH TIP!

Have your child wear the badge during dinner. They must use good manners to keep the badge and earn dessert!

You are a star player! Trace the dotted lines and then color it in.

WOW! Coach, I earned_____tickets!

(Count how many colored tickets you completed.)

You play it SMART

GAME PLAN #3 – ART OF CONVERSATION

GOAL:
With a little practice, talking with anyone can be fun and interesting. Think of it as playing tennis. Relax, serve and practice.

Coach, please read each statement aloud. Then have your child place a check in the box or color the box.

Player Mission:
☐ Use your magic words.
☐ Watch your body language and tone.
☐ Be kind and considerate while talking.
☐ Practice talking to friends and family.

Game Directions:
1. Take the challenges.
2. Find the ticket on the page and color the ticket when you have completed your mission.
3. At the end of a section, you win! Cash in for the reward chosen with your coach (an adult).

Ticket Goal:_____

Game Prize:_____

MAGIC WORD HAT

In speaking, there are magic words that are important and always appropriate to use. Color your magic hat filled with polite words and phrases. How many can you use today?

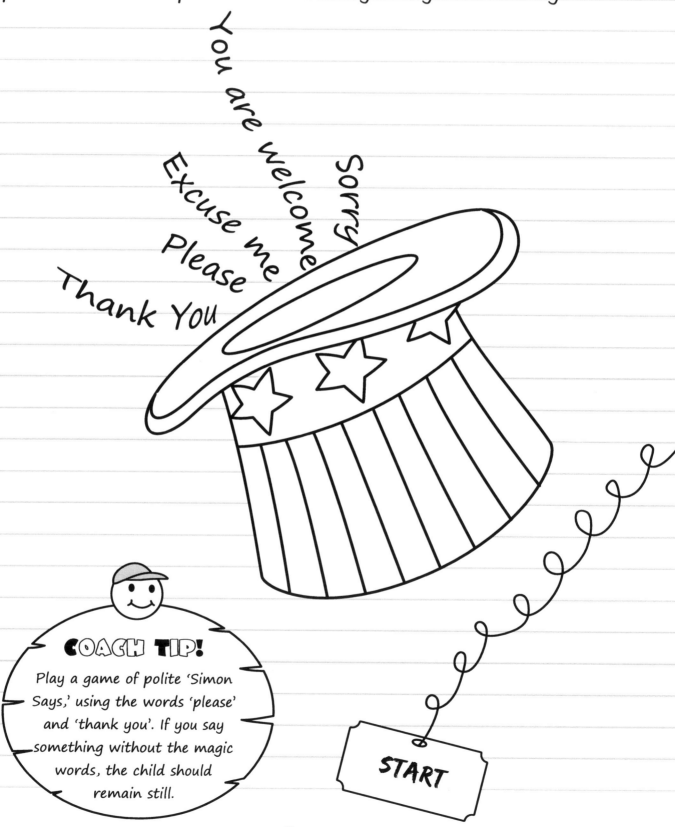

You are welcome

Sorry

Excuse me

Please

Thank You

COACH TIP!

Play a game of polite 'Simon Says,' using the words 'please' and 'thank you'. If you say something without the magic words, the child should remain still.

START

EXCUSE ME DETECTIVE

What should you say if you bump into someone? To find the answer, cross out the lower-case letters below. The letters that remain will spell a magic word.

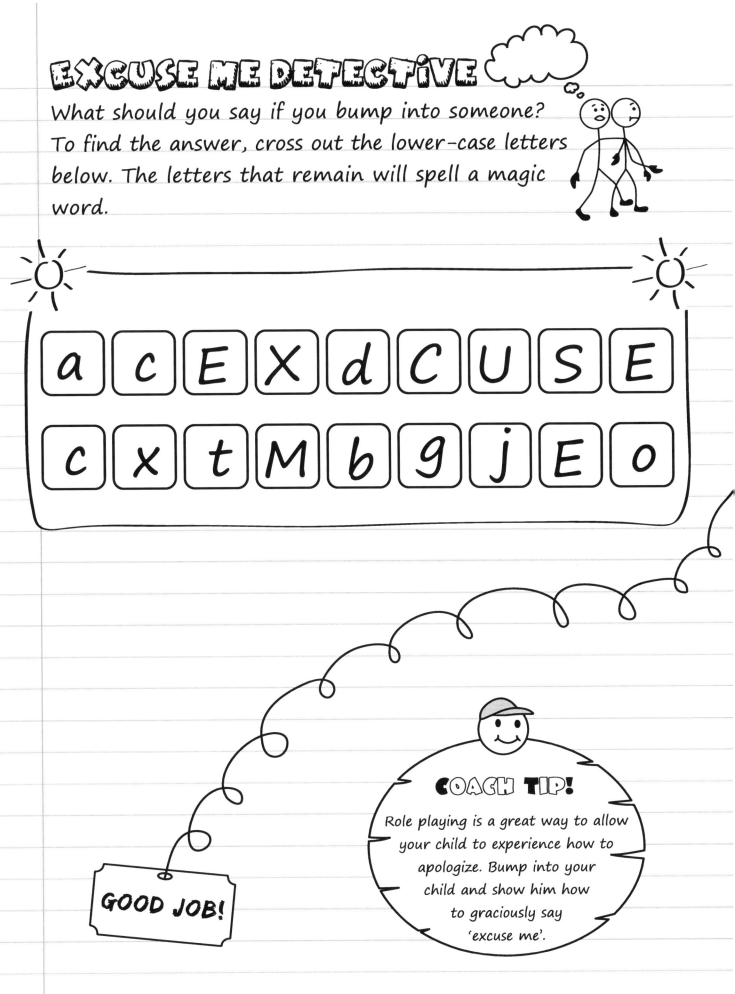

a c E X d C U S E

c x t M b g j E O

GOOD JOB!

COACH TIP!

Role playing is a great way to allow your child to experience how to apologize. Bump into your child and show him how to graciously say 'excuse me'.

MATCH THE EMOTION

Watch your tone when speaking. Please match up all the same emotions.

HAPPY!

COACH TIP!

Play 'Guess The Emotion' with your child. Have them act out being bored, angry, surprised, sad, happy and more.

42

i RICA YOU 👁

Always look people in the eye while talking. Learn the RICA rule: respect, interest, care and appreciate. Please color in the word **RICA**.

RESPECT
Earn respect by looking people in the eye

INTEREST
Eye contact tells the other person that you are interested in what they are saying.

CARE
Eye contact shows that you care what they are saying.

APPRECIATE
A meaningful look into someone's eyes says that you really mean it.

YOU GOT IT!

MY SPACE

A comfortable conversation takes place in a comfortable place. What is your comfortable space? Draw a line from the stick figure to the space that represent how comfortable you feel talking to them.

Most   Least

Mom & Dad   Stranger   Brother & Sister   Teacher

WAY TO GO!

FUMBLES AND FILLERS

Sometimes when your brain is searching for the next words to say, your mouth keeps going and blurts out meaningless words or sounds. Ready to decorate your special badge and help stop fumbles and fillers?

STOP FUMBLES AND FILLERS

COACH TIP!

Challenge your child to become a fumble & filler catcher! Who can they catch using these words?

YES!

EMPATHY DETECTIVE

Empathy is the ability to understand how someone else is feeling. Ready to detect feelings? Draw the mouth and write down the feeling.

HAPPY ☺	SAD ☹	ANGRY ><	SURPRISED :O

He feels_____

He feels_____

He feels_____

He feels_____

ALMOST THERE

TALKING TENNIS MATCH

A conversation is like a tennis ball going back and forth. You take turns. Listen. Be yourself and don't interrupt. Please trace the circles and color the tennis balls yellow. Ready to play?

ALMOST THERE

COACH TIP!

Try the DIY Conversation Cards on page 107. This is a great way to practice conversational skills with your child.

SPEAK UP!

When you talk, speak clearly and loud enough so that everyone can understand what you are saying. Please trace the missing numbers on the phone. Say the numbers aloud.

COACH TIP!

Play the telephone game. Come up with a sentence and see what happens as you whisper it from person to person. Explain how important it is to speak clearly.

AWESOME

LISTEN UP

It is always important to use your listening ears. Please follow the numbers to help create ears.

TAKE TURNS

When having a conversation it is important to take turns. It is like a ball going back and forth. Please connect the ball alphabetically, going back and forth.

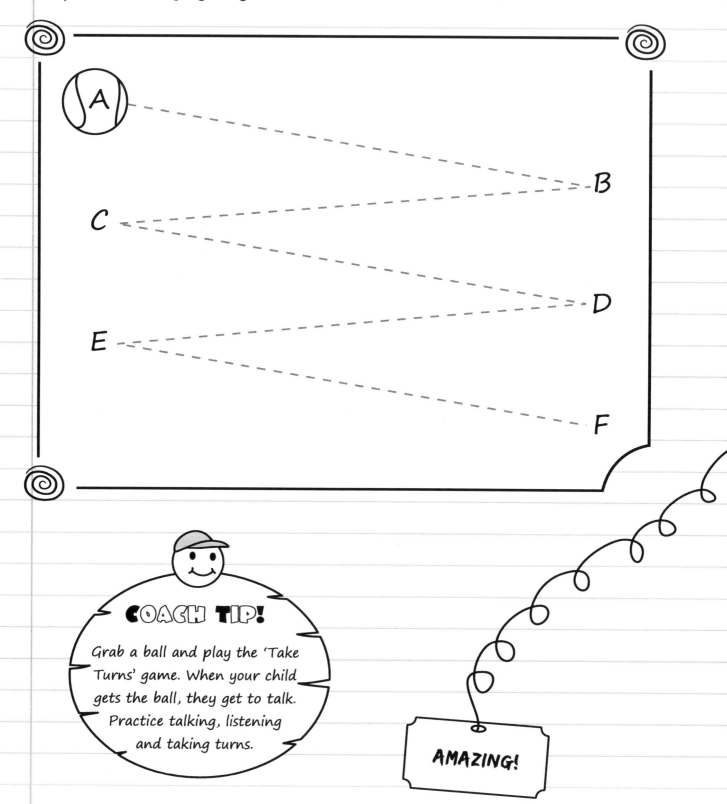

COACH TIP!

Grab a ball and play the 'Take Turns' game. When your child gets the ball, they get to talk. Practice talking, listening and taking turns.

AMAZING!

VOICE VOLUME CONTROL

Think of your voice as a thermometer. When calm, your voice volume is low. If you are very excited and upset, your volume can rise. Please help color the thermometer: 1-5 blue and 5-10 red.

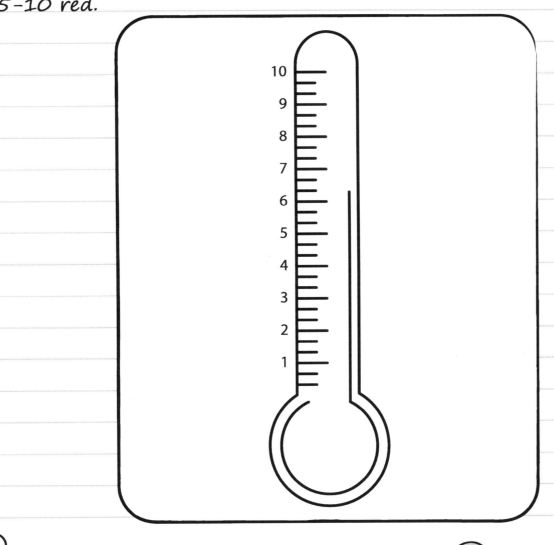

ONE MORE!

COACH TIP!

Give your child different situations and ask them to determine if we talk soft, normal or loud (i.e. library, school bus, lunch room, outside, etc.)

MIRROR, MIRROR ON THE WALL

The best way to recognize how someone is feeling is to read their face and listen to what they are saying. Draw something in the mirror that makes you excited!

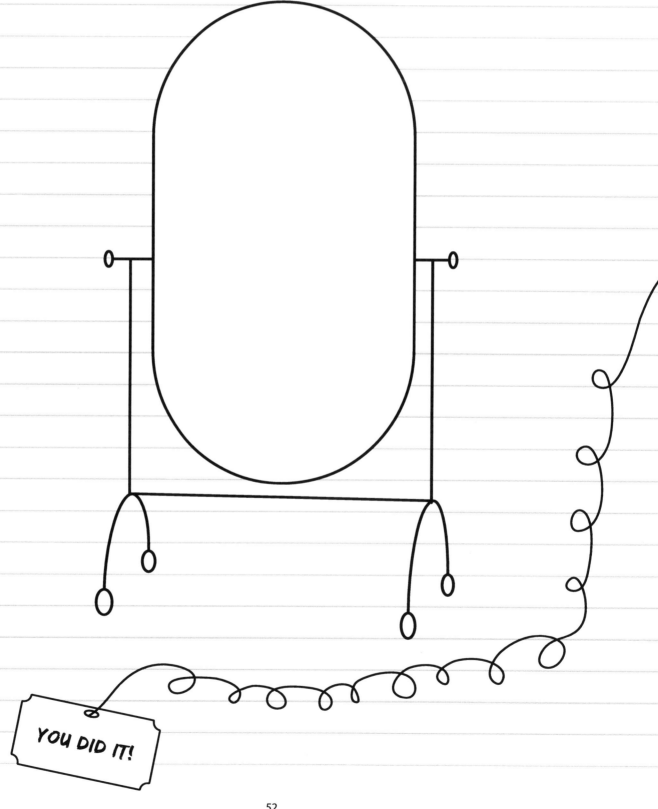

YOU DID IT!

WAY TO GO!

You are a star player! Trace the dotted lines and then color it in.

WOW! Coach, I earned _____ tickets!

(Count how many colored tickets you completed.)

You play it SMART

GAME PLAN #4 - RESTAURANT BEHAVIOR

GOAL:
We always need to show kindness and consideration to others when at a restaurant.

Coach, please read each statement aloud. Then, have your child place a check in the box or color the box.

Player Mission:
- ☐ Have good manners when eating out.
- ☐ Dress appropriately when dining out.
- ☐ Be kind and considerate to everyone in the restaurant.
- ☐ Be grateful for a special meal.

Game Directions:
1. Take the challenges.
2. Find the ticket on the page and color the ticket when you have completed your mission.
3. At the end of a section, you win! Cash in for the reward chosen with your coach (an adult).

Ticket Goal:_____

Game Prize:_____

THE DRESS CODE

What you wear makes a statement about yourself and affects how other people see you. What should he wear to a fancy restaurant? Please draw a line to help dress him.

GOOD JOB!

A FANCY CLOSET!

Please help color this fancy closet.

COACH TIP!

Play dress up with your Lil' Champ. Help your child understand how to dress for the right occasion.

GOOD JOB!

MATCH THE CLOTHES

Draw a line to match the clothing item.

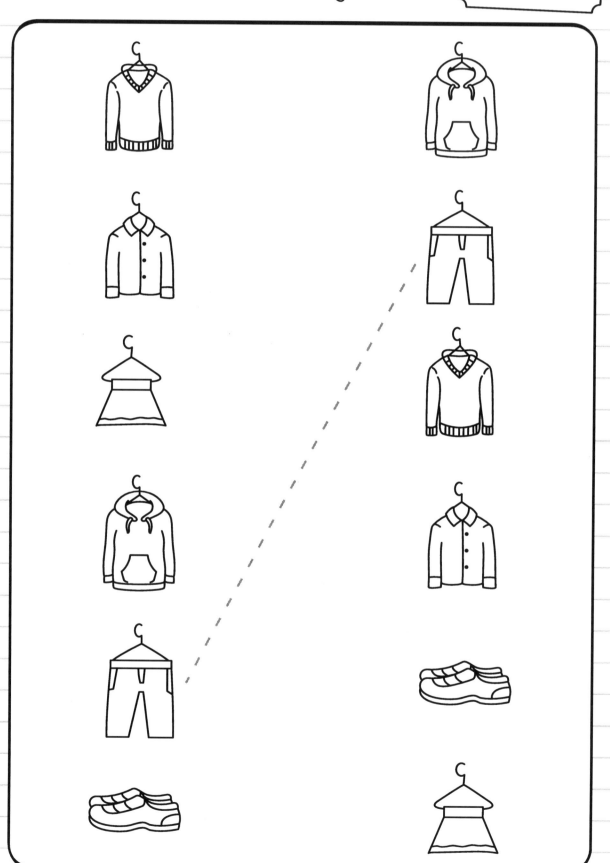

HERE i COME!

All dressed up and ready to go to a special dinner with his family. Help him find his way.

START

FINISH

WAY TO GO!

FINGER FOOD DETECTIVE

Certain foods are more challenging to eat than others. Only some foods are acceptable to eat with our fingers. Circle all of the finger foods.

Corn on the cob

Hamburger

Hot Dog

Pizza

Spaghetti

YES!

COACH TIP!

Have your child help you create a finger food party. This is a good opportunity to point out which foods are acceptable to eat with your fingers.

MY FAVORITE FOODS

Going out to eat is always a treat. We need to be thankful and grateful for this special meal. Ready to draw your favorite foods on this plate?

COACH TIP!

Begin to encourage your child to use utensils as soon as they show interest. By the age of five, you should be able to practice on a regular basis. Be patient!

AWESOME!

WHAT'S ON YOUR MENU?

In a restaurant, a menu organizes the food into different courses. You sometimes begin with an appetizer or starter, then follow with the entrée and finally a delicious dessert. Please draw a menu for dinner.

MENU

PERFECT!

COACH TIP!

Have your child help decide the dinner menu. Then he can create colorful menus for the table.

HOW TO ORDER YOUR MEAL?

When ordering your meal, make a decision, speak clearly and use the magic words! Please color the picture and then add a little magic to the order. Use these polite words: **please and thank you!**

A JOKE FOR YOU!

Question: What sport does a waiter love?

Answer: Tennis, because they can serve so well.

SIDE NOTE: Be respectful and courteous to everyone that works in the restaurant and to the people around you.

YOU CAN DO IT!

A SPECIAL DATE

Read each sentence. Circle the picture that matches.

1. Lil' Champ woke up with a smile because he had remembered he had a special date with Mom today!

2. Lil' Champ and Mom are going to a fancy restaurant.

3. Lil' Champ dresses up in fancy clothes.

4. Lil' Champ uses good table manners at the restaurant.

5. Lil' Champ is very happy!

WAY TO GO!

You are a star player! Trace the dotted lines and then color it in.

Restaurant Behavior

WOW! Coach, I earned_____tickets!

(Count how many colored tickets you completed.)

THE GOLDEN TICKET

1234891012   1234891012

You play it SMART

GAME PLAN #5 - TECHNOLOGY TALK

GOAL:

Be a great digital citizen! We need to stay safe, be respectful, and remember to enjoy life without technology too.

Coach, please read each statement aloud. Then have your child place a check in the box or color the box.

Player Mission:

- ☐ Ask permission before using technology.
- ☐ Respect time limits.
- ☐ Use the pause button.
- ☐ Be careful with your stuff.
- ☐ Enjoy other fun activities.

Game Directions:

1. Take the challenges.
2. Find the ticket on the page and color the ticket when you have completed your mission.
3. At the end of a section, you win! Cash in for the reward chosen with your coach (an adult).

Ticket Goal:_____

Game Prize:_____

THE KEY TO COMPUTER SAFETY

Your parents and teachers help you to determine which sites are educational, safe and fun! Please color your giant internet safety key!

BE A GOOD DIGITAL CITIZEN

Please draw a self-portrait under the bubble.

VOLUME CONTROL

You might love to play your favorite video, but keep in mind that there are wrong and right places to do so. Please limit the noise level in a public place. Please color the boxes by the letters. A – Blue and B – Red.

AWESOME!

COACH TIP!
Demonstrate to your child what an appropriate volume is in different situations (in their room, on a train, in a park, etc.)

HiT THE PAUSE BUTTON, PLEASE!

Pause the game, television or music when others would like to talk to you or if someone new walks into the room. Please circle the correct way to use electronics. Then color the pause button.

A

B

WAY TO GO!

GOOD DIGITAL CITIZEN DETECTIVE

There are two important words to remember as you use technology. To find the answer, cross out the lower-case letters below. The letters that remain will spell the magic words.

S c a A b F v h E

AND

R a E i S P E a C o T

YES!

COACH TIP!

Play the 'No Tech Zone' game. At a family gathering, create a basket where all the guests and family members have to leave their electronics in the basket.

FINDING MY TECH WAY

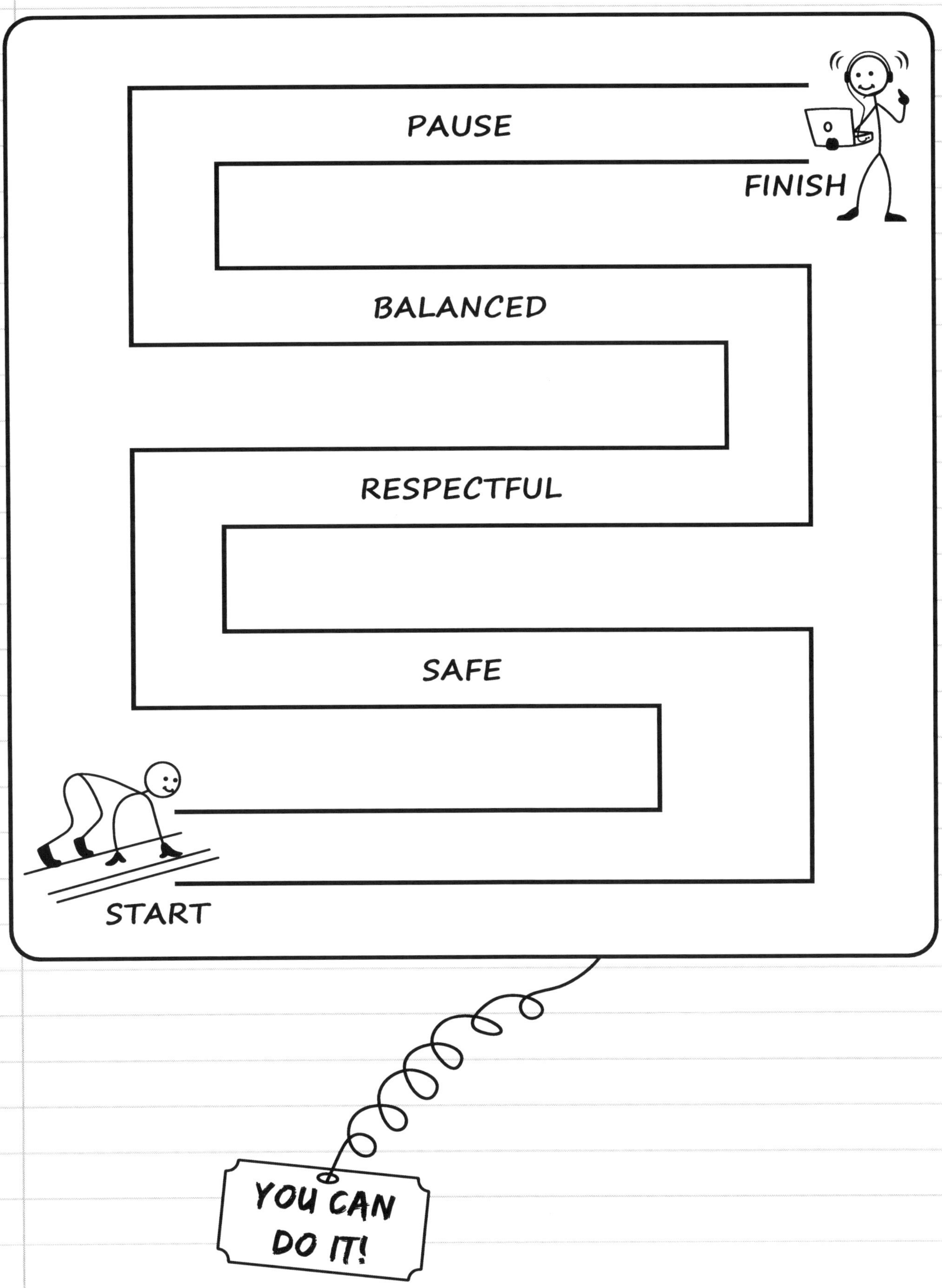

PAUSE

BALANCED

RESPECTFUL

SAFE

FINISH

START

YOU CAN DO IT!

¡ LOVE TECHNOLOGY!

Draw your favorite game or television show on the iPad.

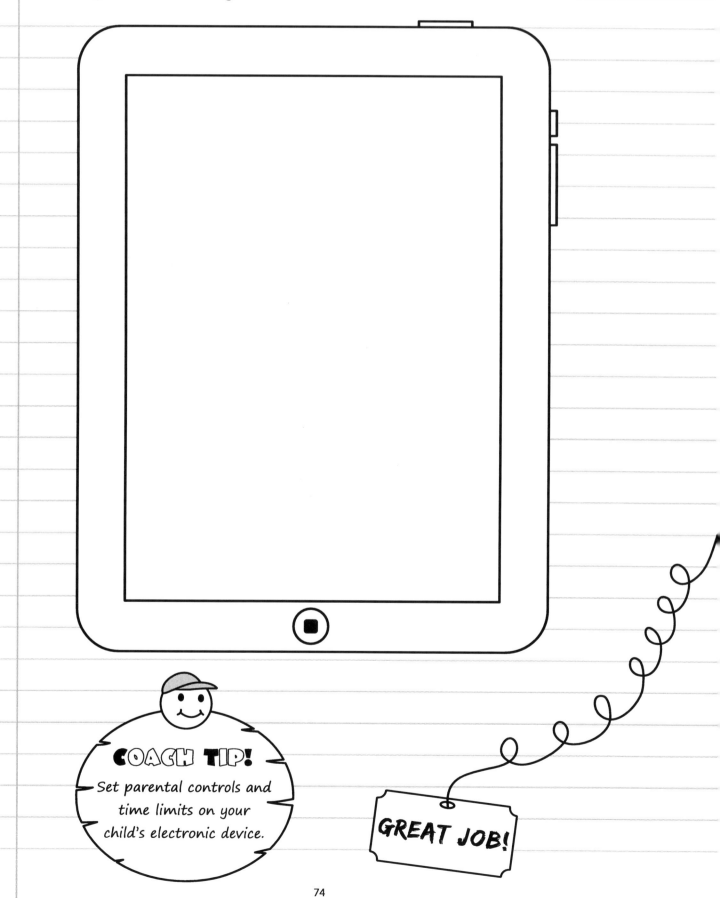

COACH TIP!

Set parental controls and time limits on your child's electronic device.

GREAT JOB!

WHAT DOESN'T BELONG?

Please circle the items that don't belong in this group.

ALMOST THERE!

TAKE CARE OF YOUR ELECTRONICS!

Please find a safe place to store your electronic gadgets.

Draw a line to all the items that belong in a special safe place.

ALMOST THERE!

A TECH JOKE FOR YOU!

Limit electronics today and add a smile to someone's day by sharing a joke. Color the picture.

YOU DID IT!

Knock, Knock!

-Who's there?

Radio

-Radio who?

Radio not, here I come!

BALANCE YOUR TIME

Technology is a lot of fun, but make an effort to balance your time. Don't forget to read books, go outside, use your imagination, and enjoy real sports and nature. Ready to use your imagination? Doodle your favorite outside sport or activity.

ALMOST THERE!

You are a star player! Trace the dotted lines and then color it in.

Technology Talk

WOW! Coach, I earned_____tickets!

(Count how many colored tickets you completed.)

You *play* it SMART

79

THE POLITE PUPPET

What you'll need: Craft stick, scissors, markers and glue. Color. Cut out face and arms and legs. Glue pieces to a craft stick. Use your polite puppet to role play situations in which manners are important. For example, how to use the words "thank you" and "please," sharing toys, giving compliments and more.

A SMART DIE GAME

What you'll need: scissors, markers and glue.

Decorate each square. Ask a parent to help you cut out the die and glue it together. Then play the SMART die game. Roll it and see what letter it lands on. Come up with one good manner or social skill that starts with the corresponding letter.

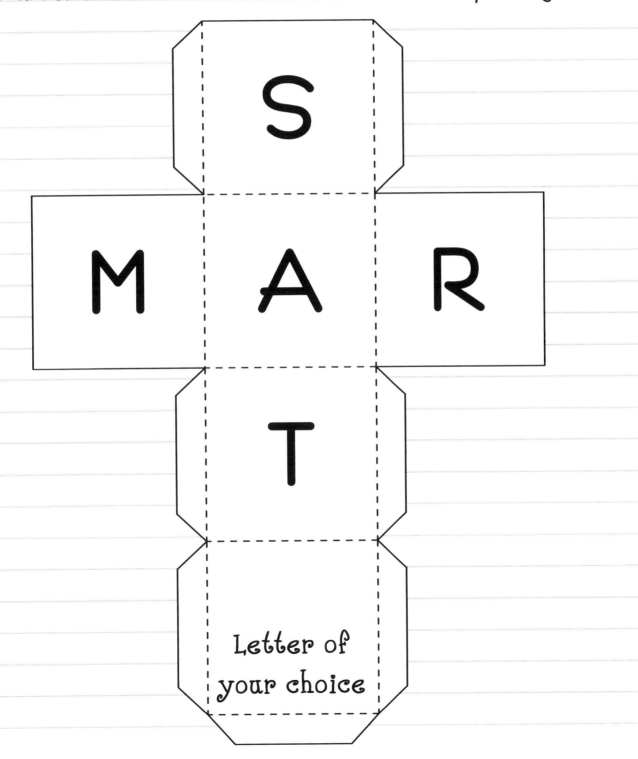

S

M A R

T

Letter of your choice

SMART MEAL MISSION

Pull out your SMART board during dinner. Ask your child to complete all the challenges. All winners get a yummy dessert!

WHO'S ON YOUR THANK LIST?

Have your parents help you write a list of anyone and everything that you are thankful for. Then draw and send them a thank you picture!

I am thankful for.....

Thank You...
....

Thank You...
....

Thank You...
....

Thank You...
....

Thank You...
....

GOOD MANNERS SECRET AGENT

Cut out secret agent manners cards. In the beginning of the meal, distribute the cards. This is your table manners mission. Don't tell anyone what is on your card. At the end of the meal, guess the manner assigned.

Place napkin on lap.

Take small bites. Keep mouth closed.

Wait until everyone is seated to start.

Wipe your lips with a napkin.

Sit up straight and remain seated.

Elbows off table.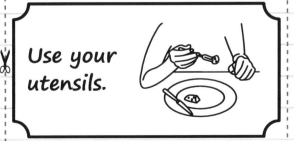

Say please and thank you throughout the meal.

Use your utensils.

ACTS OF KINDNESS MISSION

Follow the tickets and complete the challenges. Check off each mission when it's completed.

ART OF CONVERSATION MISSION

Follow the tickets and complete the challenges. Check off each mission when it's completed.

Ready for Your Mission? Art of Conversation

Play it SMART

THE GOLDEN TICKET — Ask an open-ended question.

THE GOLDEN TICKET — Say 'I like baseball' three ways – happy, sad and bored.

THE GOLDEN TICKET — Identify your comfortable personal space distance.

THE GOLDEN TICKET — Explain the word 'empathy'?

THE GOLDEN TICKET — Smile at someone today.

THE GOLDEN TICKET — Start a conversation with someone. Topic: favorite movie.

THE GOLDEN TICKET — Introduce someone today. Remember to use their name.

THE GOLDEN TICKET — Start a conversation with someone. Topic: favorite desserts.

THE GOLDEN TICKET — Use the magic word 'thank you' in a sentence.

THE GOLDEN TICKET — Use the magic word 'please' in a sentence.

THE GOLDEN TICKET — Explain the R.I.C.A rule?

THE GOLDEN TICKET — Use good eye contact while talking to a friend.

THE GOLDEN TICKET — Give someone a compliment today.

THE GOLDEN TICKET — Let's play charades! Strike the pose bored, happy and angry.

THE GOLDEN TICKET

FINISH

START

THE DO OR DON'T GAME

You make the call! Cut out the cards and play with your family.

Your friend just tripped. You laugh at her.

Answer: Don't. Your friend is probably a little embarrassed. Please don't make her feel worse.

Your mom walks in with a lot of grocery bags. You ignore her and continue playing.

Answer: Don't. Always hit the pause button and offer to help your mom.

You just got a present from your friend. You have the same one at home. You don't let her know and still thank her for the great gift.

Answer: Do. Yes, always say something positive when you receive a gift.

You rush to go through the door but slow down when you realize someone is behind you. You decide to help open the door and let them go first.

Answer: Do. Holding a door open is always the polite way.

Your friend says "Hello" and you say "Hello" back with a smile.

Answer: Do. Always say "Hello" back with a smile.

You go to your friend's house and begin jumping on her couch.

Answer: Don't. A good guest respects the rules of the house and should not jump on other people's furniture.

93

You are upset because you didn't score a goal in soccer. You take your ball and throw it away.

Answer: Don't. Always show good sportsmanship.

Your grandmother sent a great gift and you decide to send her a thoughtful thank-you note.

Answer: Do. Always write a polite thank-you note.

You tell your mom what happened in school while playing on your iPad.

Answer: Don't. Please put the iPad away and talk to your mom face-to-face.

Your friend just came to your party and gave you a gift. You grab it and give her a nod.

Answer: Don't. Remember to always say "thank you."

Your brother apologized for breaking your new video game. You reply, "Okay, I forgive you."

Answer: Do. Remember to forgive with grace.

You bump into someone in the hallway and she trips. You yell, "Hey! Watch where you are going!"

Answer: Don't. Remember to say "Excuse me."

Jane meets Joe for the first time. She smiles brightly, stands tall and introduces herself.

Answer: Do. Remember to use your smile and introduce yourself.

Nicky talks to Annie while looking down at his feet.

Answer: Don't. Remember the RICA rule! Always look people in the eye while speaking.

Sandy is sharing a story with a friend. She says, "Um, uh, Jane would like, you know, to share a, like, story with her class. What I'm trying to say...."

Answer: Don't. Remember the fumble and filler police. Avoid using words that don't mean anything.

You are talking in a large group of kids. John is talking about soccer. Jill doesn't understand the rules of soccer. She is feeling left out. You try to include her in the conversation.

Answer: Do. Remember to always try to make others feel comfortable.

You would like to have more cookies for dessert. You say, "I want more cookies."

Answer: Don't. Remember to ask politely, "May I please have another cookie?"

You chew with your mouth open.

Answer: Don't. Always take small bites and keep your mouth closed.

You rest your elbows on the table while eating.

Answer: Don't. No elbows on the table while eating, please!

You wipe your mouth with a napkin.

Answer: Do. Always use your napkin. Please, no sleeves!

You make loud noises while eating.

Answer: Don't. No one wants to hear your slurping or burping noises.

You are bored and decide to eat and play with your toys at the table.

Answer: Don't. Please, no toys at the table.

You prefer to use your fingers while eating.

Answer: Don't. Please use your fork or spoon. Reserve the fingers for only certain finger foods!

You decide to throw your iPad on the floor instead of putting it away in a safe place.

Answer: Don't. Please be careful with your electronics and find a safe place to use and store them.

WOULD YOU RATHER.....

Making conversation with someone new can be fun. How about a quick game of "Would you rather...." to practice. Remember to ask "why".

.....................play
in the snow
or jump in
puddles in
the rain?

.....................have
well-mannered
dog or a
crazy monkey?

.....................give
or get a
present?

MAGIC WORD CARDS

Cut out the cards. Turn them over so you can't see what they are. Pick a card and make up a sentence using the word on it.

THANK YOU

PLEASE

I AM SORRY

MAY I PLEASE HAVE...

EXCUSE ME

AFTER YOU, PLEASE

GUESS THE EMOTION

Cut out the cards. Turn them over so you can't see what they are. Then turn over one card and pretend to be an animal using the emotion shown. For example, you might have to be a happy dog.

HAPPY

SAD

SURPRISED

ANGRY

DIY CONVERSATION CARDS

Perk up your family talk! Just cut out the cards. Create the family talk jar. One person picks a card and everyone can answer the same question or everyone can pick their own. Listen and take turns.

SEASONS OF THE YEAR

What is your favorite season? Why? Do you know an interesting fact about your favorite season? Name a fun family activity during this season?

FAVORITE SPORTS

What is your favorite sport? Who is your favorite player? Who is your favorite team? What's an interesting fact?

PLAN A DREAM VACATION

Where would you go on a dream vacation? Who would come? What would you do? Why? What's an interesting fact about your choice?

FAVORITE CANDY

What type of candy do you like to eat? What would happen if you ate tons of candy every day?

EXERCISE IMPORTANT

Why should we exercise? What are some forms of exercising? How many times a week should we exercise? What is your favorite type of exercise? What is your least favorite exercise?

SUPERPOWERS

If you could have any superpower, which would you choose? Why?

ANIMAL

If you could be an animal, what would you be and why?

YOUR FAVORITE THING

What is one thing you couldn't live without? Why?

FAME FOR 10 SECONDS

If you had the attention of the world for 10 seconds, what would you say? Why?

BEST HOLIDAY

What is your favorite holiday to celebrate? Why?

INTERESTING FACTS ABOUT YOU

Name three interesting things about you?

TEACH A CLASS FOR A DAY

If you had to teach a class for a day, what subject would you choose? What would you do?

DIY CONVERSATION CARDS

Make your own cards.

THE GIGGLE JAR

Promote smiles and giggles! Cut out the cards and place in a jar. Then keep adding new ones with the blank cards. This will provide hours of entertainment and a great way to put a smile on your lil' champ's face.

Why is 6 scared of 7?
Because 7, "8", 9!

Knock Knock!
-Who's there?
Boo
-Boo who?
Well you don't need to cry about it.

Knock, Knock!
-Who's there?
Cowsgo
-Cowsgo who?
No they don't. Cows go moo!

Q: Which hand is better to write with?
A: Neither, it's best to write with a pen!

Q: What do you call a pig who plays basketball?
A: A ball hog!

Knock, Knock!
-Who's there?
Dishes
-Dishes me, who are you?

Knock, Knock!
-Who's there?
Dewey
-Dewey who?
Dewey have to keep telling these jokes!

Q: What do you call an elephant in a phone booth?
A: Stuck

Q: What did the angry customer give to the Italian waiter?
A: A pizza his mind.

Knock, Knock!
-Who's there?
Lettuce
-Lettuce who?
Lettuce in, we're freezing.

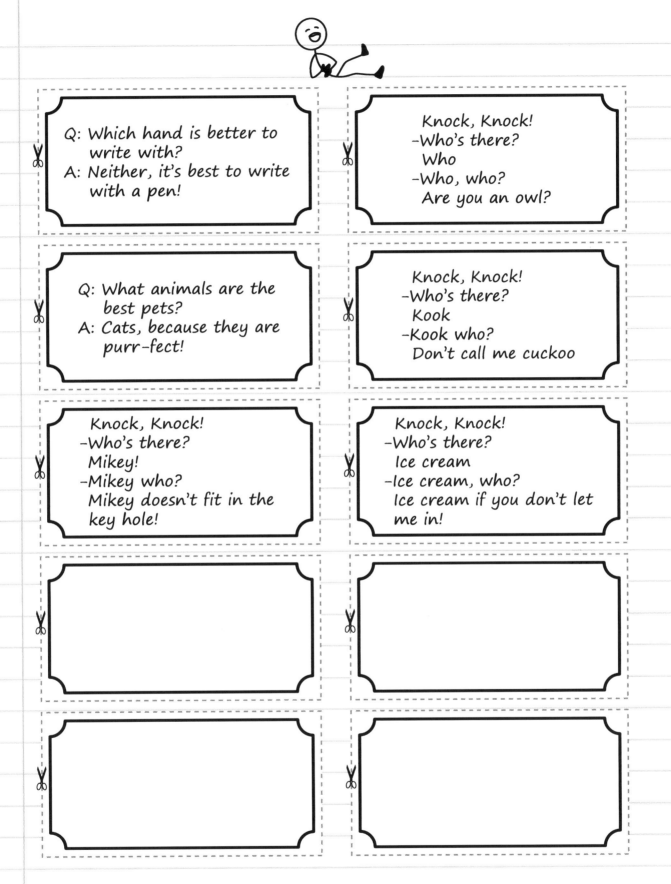

Q: Which hand is better to write with?
A: Neither, it's best to write with a pen!

Knock, Knock!
-Who's there?
Who
-Who, who?
Are you an owl?

Q: What animals are the best pets?
A: Cats, because they are purr-fect!

Knock, Knock!
-Who's there?
Kook
-Kook who?
Don't call me cuckoo

Knock, Knock!
-Who's there?
Mikey!
-Mikey who?
Mikey doesn't fit in the key hole!

Knock, Knock!
-Who's there?
Ice cream
-Ice cream, who?
Ice cream if you don't let me in!

For more ideas on jokes visit **www.thesmartplaybook.com**

113

MAKE YOUR OWN CROWN

What you'll need: Scissors, crayons and tape.

Color. Cut out crown and tape pieces together to fit around your head.

PARENT BOOK SUGGESTIONS TO READ WITH YOUR LIL' CHAMP!

- **Penguin Says Please** by Michael Dahl
- **My Manners Matter** by Pat Thomas
- **Manners** by Aliki
- **May I Please Have a Cookie** by Jennifer Morris
- **Manners at the Table** by Carrie Finn
- **Manners at the Restaurant** by Mankato Minn
- **The Cat Who Came for Tacos** by Morton Grove
- **Hands Are Not For Hitting** by Martine Agassi
- **Do Unto Others** by Laurie Keller
- **It's Mine** by Leo Lionni
- **Clifford's Birthday Party** by Norman Bridwell
- **My Mouth is a Volcano** by Julia Cook
- **The Berenstain Bears Tell The Truth** by Stan Berenstain and Jan Berenstain
- **Tattlin' Madeline** by Carol Cummings
- **Dude, That's Rude!** Pamela Espeland
- **How Kind** by Mary Murphy
- **Kindness is Cooler, Mrs. Ruler** by Mrgly Cuyler
- **An Awesome Book of Thanks** by Dallas Clayton
- **Bear Says Thank You** by Michael Dahl
- **Interrupting Chicken** by David Ezra Stein
- **Don't Let the Pigeon Drive the Bus** by Mo Willems
- **The Big Tee Ball Game** by Larry Dane Brimmer

PARENT SMART CHECKLIST

Important skills to teach, model and practice with your child, and a great reminder for the entire family.

- ☐ Use "Please" and "Thank You".
- ☐ Give a sincere apology.
- ☐ Say "Excuse Me" instead of nothing or "What".
- ☐ Share toys and play fair.
- ☐ Be a polite play date.
- ☐ Basic greetings – hello and goodbye.
- ☐ Listen and take turns while speaking.
- ☐ Be kind and respectful.
- ☐ Be helpful and compassionate.
- ☐ Voice control.
- ☐ Don't hold grudges and learn to move on.
- ☐ Dinner table manners basics – use napkin, use cutlery, chew with mouth closed, no toys at the table, sit still, thank the cook and ask to be excused.
- ☐ Dressing appropriately for different situations.
- ☐ Eating out basics.

ANSWER KEY

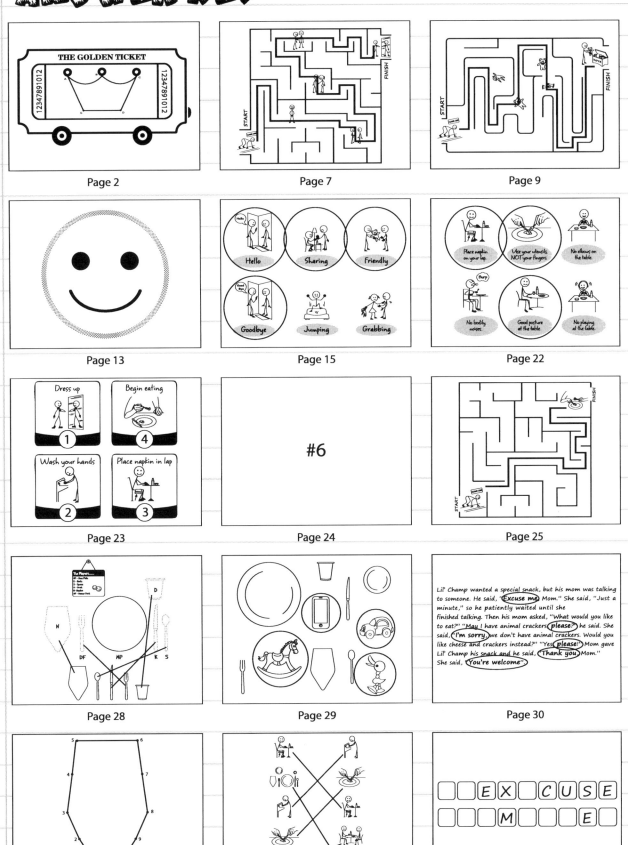

Page 2

Page 7

Page 9

Page 13

Page 15

Page 22

Page 23

#6

Page 24

Page 25

Page 28

Page 29

Lil' Champ wanted a special snack, but his mom was talking to someone. He said, "(Excuse me) Mom." She said, "Just a minute," so he patiently waited until she finished talking. Then his mom asked, "What would you like to eat?" "May I have animal crackers (please?) he said. She said, (I'm sorry,) we don't have animal crackers. Would you like cheese and crackers instead?" "Yes (please!)" Mom gave Lil' Champ his snack and he said, (Thank you) Mom." She said, (You're welcome)".

Page 30

Page 31

Page 33

Page 41

ANSWER KEY

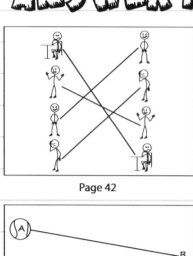

Page 42

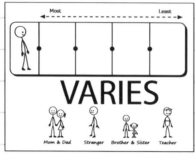

Page 44

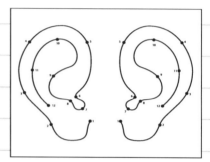

Page 49

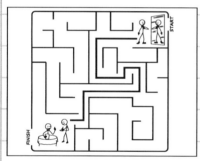

Page 50

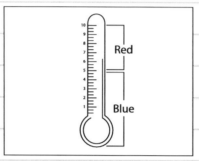

Page 51

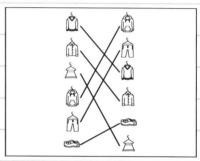

Page 58

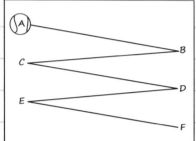

Page 59

Page 60

Page 63

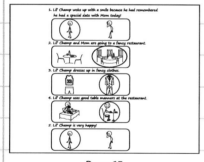

Page 65

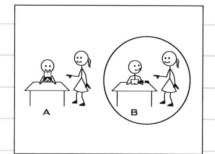

Page 71

Page 72

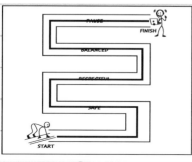

Page 73

Page 75

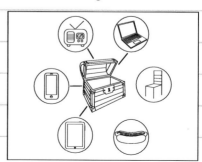

Page 76

21876292R00074

Made in the USA
Middletown, DE
14 July 2015